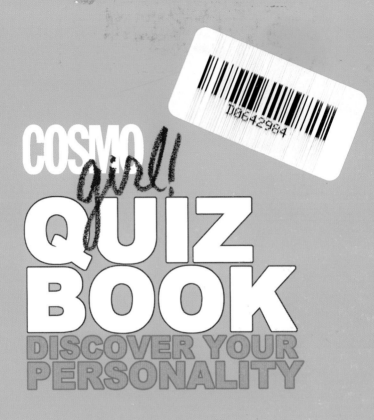

COSMO *girl!*
QUIZ
BOOK
DISCOVER YOUR PERSONALITY

COSMO girl! QUIZ BOOK

DISCOVER YOUR PERSONALITY

From the Editors of
CosmoGIRL!

Hearst Books
A Division of Sterling
Publishing Co., Inc.
New York

Library of Congress Cataloging-in-Publication Data
CosmoGirl quiz book : discover your personality / from the editors of CosmoGirl.
    p. cm.
  ISBN 1-58816-489-6
  1. Teenage girls--Psychology--Miscellanea. 2. Personality tests for youth. I. Title:
Discover your personality. II. Cosmo girl.
  HQ798.C594 2006
  305.235'2--dc22

                                    2004029401

10 9 8 7 6 5 4 3 2 1

Book design by Margaret Rubiano

Published by Hearst Books
A Division of Sterling Publishing Co., Inc.
387 Park Ave. South, New York, NY 10016

CosmoGirl! is a trademark owned by Hearst Magazines Property, Inc., in USA, and
Hearst Communications, Inc., in Canada. Hearst Books is a trademark owned by
Hearst Communications, Inc.

www.cosmogirl.com

For information about custom editions, special sales, premium and corporate purchas-
es, please contact Sterling Special Sales Department at 800-805-5489 or special-
sales@sterlingpub.com.

Distributed in Canada by Sterling Publishing
c/o Canadian Manda Group, 165 Dufferin Street
Toronto, Ontario, Canada M6K 3H6

Distributed in Australia by Capricorn Link (Australia) Pty. Ltd.

P.O. Box 704, Windsor, NSW 2756 Australia

Printed in China

ISBN: 1-58816-489-6

Photo Credits:
Cover Photo: Eri Morita

Bruno Barbazan, pg. 6, 20; Bumper, pg. 14; Alban Christ, pg. 24; Rebecca Greenfield,
pg. 109; Stephen Lee, pg. 72; Chayo Mata, pg. 80; Glynnis McDaris, pg. 78, 88; Eri
Morita, pg. 18, 36, 48, 66, 68, 94, 104; Pascal Preti, pg. 56; Saye, pg. 12, 28, 32, 46,
60, 65, 90; Cleo Sullivan, pg. 42, 84, 110, 111; Hugo Tillman, pg. 7, 8, 9, 40, 52, 100.

Contents

For Fun

From Me to You

Who are you, CosmoGIRL!? What's your cup o' joe, what kind of prom dress fits your personality, what color is your aura? These questions may seem a little silly, but if you think about them a little more, they're actually just a fun, kooky way of looking at yourself, your life—your personality. And when you answer them, they really can help you figure out who you are. It's not an easy thing to do, especially when you have so much going on in your life. You've got school, sports, after-school activities like art or music or your job; you've got friends to hang out with and be there for; you've got family responsibilities like taking care of your younger siblings or getting dinner started while your mom's on her way home from work—tons of stuff that can easily take time away from YOU. Not all of those things are bad, of course, but hey, there are only 24 hours in the day! If your time is taken up with all that other stuff, then sometimes you're the last person you think about, right?

Well, that's where this fun little handy-dandy *CosmoGIRL!* quiz book comes in. These pages are packed with tons of great quizzes (which I know you just love!) that give you the excuse to take some time to yourself to think about YOU in different ways. You'll find out about facets of your personality that you've never thought about before. You may joke around about them with your family or your friends, or you may choose never to share them with anyone else, but either way, I guarantee that these quizzes will help you know yourself better and inspire you to think in unexpected ways. Because when you look at yourself through these silly, crazy, unusual lenses, it helps you look at the world through more colorful lenses too—and that makes you feel good about yourself and the world around you.

So have fun discovering what cup o' joe, what kind of prom dress, and what color your aura is (and more!)—and don't let anyone tell you those things aren't important, you hear?! Let me know what you think of these quizzes—and if you have any quiz ideas of your own that you'd like to see in *CosmoGIRL!* magazine, drop me a line at susan@cosmogirl.com. Now I think there's a Vanilla latte waiting for me somewhere... Ha ha!

Love,

Susan

get to
know yourself

WHO ARE YOU?

Take this quiz and you can uncover the hidden powers of your personality!

Pick your answers: For each statement, give yourself 4 points for the answer that fits you best, 3 points for the next best, 2 for the third best, and 1 for the one that fits you least. (Don't worry—there are no "right" answers!)

1. In school, you enjoy:
a. History/civics.
b. Phys ed.
c. English/writing.
d. Science/math.

2. In your family, your role is the:
a. Helping hand.
b. Troublemaker.
c. Peacekeeper.
d. Voice of reason.

3. You're drawn to a guy who is:
a. Dependable and level headed.
b. Bold and free-spirited.
c. Sensitive and soulful.
d. Smart and independent.

4. Your most typical mood is:
a. Cautious and responsible.
b. Excited and stimulated.
c. Eager and motivated.
d. Calm and detached.

5. You most want to have:
a. Security.
b. Fun.
c. Self-understanding.
d. Knowledge.

6. You pride yourself on your:
a. Good judgment.
b. Creativity.
c. Ambition.
d. Competence.

7. You want to become a:
a. Good citizen.
b. Big star.
c. Well-rounded person.
d. Great genius.

8. You want others to see you as:
a. Hardworking.
b. Playful.
c. Sincere.
d. Strong-willed.

Scoring

Are you a guardian, an artisan, an idealist, or a realist? Discover your secret personality traits—and the incredible power they give you. Just add up all the *a*s, the *b*s, the *c*s, and the *d*s. Whichever letter has the highest score holds the key to uncovering your true self. Use that power to be the best you can be!

Guardian If *a* was your highest score...

Guardians are sensible, down-to-earth people who value family and give back to their community. Others depend on you to get the job done because you understand how to play by the rules—and win.

Artisan If *b* was your highest score...

Artisans are impulsive, sensual people who want to be free to do *what* they want, *how* they want. You never take no for an answer. Instead, you don't rest until you figure out how to accomplish your goals (which you always do).

Idealist If *c* was your highest score...

Idealists are imaginative, enthusiastic, ethical people who constantly analyze themselves to discover who they are. You're continually striving for self-improvement, and you never act phony and always stand by your beliefs—no matter what the risk.

Realist If *d* was your highest score...

Realists are curious, skeptical, and fiercely independent thinkers. You want to understand how things work so you can make them work even better. Instead of relying on what's already there, you push yourself until you come up with new and innovative ideas.

DISCOVER YOUR SECRET SELF!

See how the colors you choose instantly reveal the real you!

Did you know that your color preferences reveal your personality traits, like what motivates you? So clear your head and pick the first color you're drawn to. Don't think about how great you look in red—it's about your gut reaction to the colors. Choose one from the left set of colored rings below, then one from the right. Now find the analysis for your color combo and let the Dewey Color System show you what you're *really* all about.

PICK ONE OF THESE

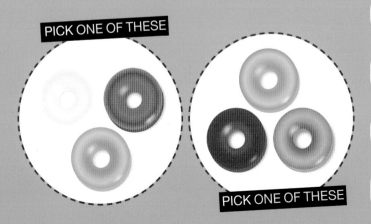

PICK ONE OF THESE

red-green
You're Miss Practical—and nothing can shake your levelheadedness. Your calm demeanor helps to keep everyone around you sane.

yellow-green
Caretaking comes naturally to you, and you feel fulfilled by it. You're the one friends always come to when they need support and a ready ear.

blue-green
Your curiosity motivates you, and you're extremely observant. You can see people's dreams and give them the self-confidence to follow through.

red-purple
Order is your middle name. You're at your best when in control or directing others, which is probably why you plan all those super events!

yellow-purple
Change fuels your inner fire, and you *live* to be on the go, exploring new places. Each new adventure brings you a stronger sense of self.

blue-purple
You're always the center of attention, and people are drawn to you. You're inspired to turn grandiose daydreams into amazing realities.

red-orange
You thrive on individuality—and never follow the crowd. You're a take-action girl who fights for those who can't express themselves as freely.

yellow-orange
You are a constant innovator who loves making something out of nothing. You're always seeking out challenges to avoid getting stuck in a rut.

blue-orange
One minute you're creative and free, the next you're all logic. This duality keeps everyone on their toes, which makes you the life of *any* party.

ARE YOU AN IT GIRL?

Pssst! There's a new girl who's stepping into the spotlight. Could she be you?
Take this quick quiz to find out!

Answer true or false to each statement below, then tally your score to see if you put the *isma* in *charisma!*

1. My friends frequently come to me seeking my advice for their problems.

   TRUE ___
   FALSE ___

2. When I meet new people, my mind doesn't wander off. I'm usually really interested.

   TRUE ___
   FALSE ___

3. I try to put people at ease. It doesn't matter who they are—I think it's best when people are comfortable around me.

   TRUE ___
   FALSE ___

4. I get excited about many of the same things that excite my friends.

   TRUE ___
   FALSE ___

5. I can find something to like about almost everyone I meet, even if it's a little thing.

   TRUE ___
   FALSE ___

6. I don't worry a lot about the impression that I make on other people. I'm pretty confident that I give off a good vibe.

   TRUE ___
   FALSE ___

7. People notice that I'm usually in high spirits.

TRUE ⊠
FALSE ____

8. The way I see it, most people have a lot to say—and I'm happy to hear it.

TRUE ⊠
FALSE ____

9. Most of my friends would be surprised to find that I have problems just like theirs.

TRUE ____
FALSE ⊠

10. I like it when people share with me the little details of their lives. It's what makes them interesting and unique!

TRUE ⊠
FALSE ____

Give yourself one point for every time you answered TRUE. TOTAL ____

HOW MANY POINTS DID YOU SCORE?

8-10 points: you've got it

People gravitate toward you because you have that gift of making them feel at ease. That's why you have tons of friends!

5-7 points: you're working on it

You know how to tune in to others' good qualities, so make an effort to show off *yours*, and you're sure to become It.

1-4 points: you could use more of it

You're an amazing person—so let people in on the secret! Hint: Try starting a conversation by complimenting someone. It works!

Find out more about the simple secrets of charismatic people!

Girls with the most charisma would answer true to every question. Here's why:
(1) A charismatic person is a nonjudgmental confidant—her friends trust her.
(2) She pays attention to people and (3) cares about making them feel relaxed around her.
(4) She's enthusiastic about the things that make her friends feel good, (5) is friendly and outgoing, (6) and acts self-assured by not obsessing about what others think of her.
(7) She's upbeat and positive, and (8) enjoys conversation. (9) She seems worry-free, even though she has issues like everyone else. (10) People can talk to her about anything—she's genuinely interested in others' stories.

DISCOVER YOUR INNER GODDESS

Thought mythology was boring? Take our quiz and think again!

Directions and scoring:
Read each pair of statements and choose the one that describes you best.

1. a. I think that I'm more of a dreamer than practical.
   b. I think that I'm more practical than a dreamer.

2. a. I like variety in life more than a regular routine.
   b. I prefer to stick with things I already know how to do.

3. a. I think most issues have many different sides.
   b. Most issues have two sides—a right and a wrong one.

4. a. I love to think up new ways to do things.
   b. I like to do things the way they've always worked.

5. c. I'm the type who analyzes situations and problems.
   d. I'm more of a "doer" than a "thinker."

6. c. My head usually rules my heart.
   d. I make decisions based mostly on my feelings.

7. c. I always do more work than what's asked of me.
   d. I do just enough work to get by.

8. c. I'd rather compete than collaborate as a group.
   d. I'd rather collaborate than compete.

Add up how many A's, B's, C's, and D's you picked. The two most common letters in your results will reveal your goddess sister, below.

A+C Artemis

Just like Artemis, you're a natural-born leader who hits whatever target you aim for. You're as brave as they come and are always willing to fight for what you believe in. Being a leader comes easy for you because you see the big picture and aren't afraid to make tough decisions. But sometimes you do forget to include others in your plans or to get their support, so try to remember that the people around you are there to help—and they probably have great ideas too!

A+D Psyche

The most mystical of goddesses, Psyche continually searches for insight and purpose in her life, and so do you. It's that curiosity, creativity, and sense of wonder that help you to keep growing as a person. And because you're so sensitive to what's going on around you, you easily pick up on other people's moods and provide a great shoulder to cry on. But trying to help everyone out all the time can get overwhelming, so find time to focus on your needs and pamper yourself once in a while.

B+C Athena

You, Athena girl, are wise beyond your years! With your knowledge and strong desire to succeed, you master whatever you set out to do. It may take longer than you'd like, since you carefully think things through, but it always gets done— thanks to your steady determination. Just be careful: Your combination of drive and logic can lead you to believe you're always right. Try to take other people's feelings into consideration before you automatically dismiss their ideas.

B+D Aphrodite

As an Aphrodite girl, you shine in the spotlight and always have admirers. That's because you take advantage of all that life has to offer by living in the moment, trying new things, and making sure everyone around you is having fun too. But when things get gloomy, you tend to take off for brighter surroundings. Instead of running away, make an effort to deal with any unpleasantness head on—once you actively try to work it out, you'll see how strong and capable you really are!

DO PEOPLE GET YOU?

Find out if you're a good communicator—and how to become one if you're not!

1. When a friend asks you to lie to her mom on her behalf, it makes you uncomfortable, so you:

a. Say, "Uh, um...yeah, sure. Whatever."
b. Say, "Okay" but let your phone go to voice mail when her mom actually calls.
c. Say, "I'm not comfortable doing that."

2. Your mom asks you to describe the dress you fell in love with at the mall. You say:

a. "It was, like, pink with, like, a black satin, ya know, bow around the waist."
b. "It was pink with, like, a black satin bow around the waist."
c. "It was pink with a black satin bow around the waist."

3. A close friend said she'd call you back, but she didn't. When you see her in school the next day:

a. You pretend like everything's fine, even though you're sort of hurt.
b. You give her one-word answers so she'll get the hint and ask if you're mad.
c. You say, "You never called me back last night. What happened?"

4. Now that you think about it, who's doing most of the talking in your everyday conversations?

a. You; your friends and family actually tease you about your *loooong* stories.
b. The other person; you respond, but you're not much of a conversation starter.
c. It's balanced; you and the other person both talk— and listen.

5. You don't want to cover your coworker's shift when your boss asks if you're able to, so you say:

a. "If you really need me, I guess I can."
b. "I actually already made other plans that I can't get out of."
c. "I'm sorry, but I can't that day."

6. You're talking to your teacher about an assignment. What is your body language like?

a. You have your arms crossed.
b. You're waving your hands around to drive home the point you're making.
c. You're leaning in toward her.

7. You're talking to your crush, and you disagree with something he says about animal rights. You:

a. Act like you agree so he won't think you're argumentative or something.
b. Casually change the topic and hope he doesn't bring it up again.
c. Tell him that you see his point, but you think [your opinion here!].

8. When your teacher calls on you in class, are you able to look her in the eye?

a. No, not really.
b. Sometimes.
c. Yeah. Why wouldn't I be?

Scoring

Check the letter you picked the most to see if you communicate well!

A Well, uh, no.

You're not clear with people about what you want or think. Each time you hold yourself back from saying what you mean, write down how you *wish* you'd handled the situation. Then you can try to do *that* the next time!

B Sort of...sometimes.

When you're comfortable, you're clear. But if you're intimidated, you get tongue-tied. Next time you feel awkward saying what you think, force yourself to *speak up*. It may feel unnatural, but you'll build the skill—and your confidence.

C Definitely yes.

Your directness will help you forge solid relationships now and in the future! Be sure that you also let others say what they need to—and that you *think* about their point before responding. That way, you'll get them as much as they get you!

ARE YOU A STRESS CASE?

Midterm! Crush! Curfew! Okay, take five minutes out of your life for this quiz—you may need it more than you know.

Add up the points of every statement that applies to your life over the past six months.

1. You got your driver's license (yahoo!) and started driving on your own. (20 points) _____

2. You often feel guilty or nervous about something. (25 points) _____

3. You have unexplained stomachaches or headaches at least twice a week. (25 points each) _____

4. You tend to blush or sweat more than usual in social situations. (25 points) _____

5. You have a harder time sleeping than normal or have a lot of nightmares. (25 points) _____

6. Your looks have changed (not just a haircut—more like a big change in weight). (30 points) _____

7. You've gotten into a new relationship or ended one you had. (35 points) _____

8. You applied to college (or you're in the process of applying right now). (40 points) _____

9. You've had lots of problems with your grades or with one particular teacher. (45 points) _____

10. You're taking Advanced Placement or honors classes. (45 points) _____

11. You do after-school activities that take up at least 10 hours a week. (45 points) _____

12. You and your family have moved to a different city. (65 points) _____

13. A new baby brother or sister has entered your family. (70 points) _____

14. Your parents got divorced or decided to separate. (80 points) _____

15. You got pregnant without wanting to or meaning to. (80 points) _____

16. A parent (100 points), sibling (95 points), or best friend (90 points) died. _____

Your Scorecard

over 200 points: HIGH

You're under a lot of stress, but try not to feel hopeless. Stress is about how in-control you feel. So, put your stresses into two lists: "things I can change" (college stress) and "things I can't" (your parents' divorce). Take charge of the "can't" list by talking to a counselor (even *asking* for help puts you in control). And for the "can" list, make a de-stressing plan. Maybe map out a college application schedule to break up the process into manageable chunks (college visits, essay due dates).

100-200 point: MEDIUM

You are definitely stressed, whether it's because of a major life-changing event or just a hectic schedule. You need to stop and smell the mocha latte, and make downtime a *priority*. Here's how: Schedule two hours each week in your planner for something relaxing. Some people like physical stuff, like running, but you could also bake cookies or even read romance novels—whatever *calms* you. And the next time anyone asks you to take on a stressful task, tell them your schedule's *full*.

Under 100 points: LOW

You're in control, girl. You've been lucky not to have been through many earth-shattering events lately, and if little stuff's come up, you've dealt and avoided stress symptoms. That'll make you healthier for *life*. You're in such good shape, you could benefit from challenging yourself. Think of something scary you've wanted to do (like running for class office), and let that stress motivate you to take the risk. What feels like fear might *actually* be your inner spirit chanting, "Go for it!"

WHAT'S YOUR SECRET STRENGTH?

You have a superpower. Oh, yes you do! Now, find it!

1. When you get older, you'll be:
a. An actor.
b. A detective.
c. An ad exec.
d. A firefighter.

2. If you were a pair of shoes you'de be:
a. Simple black flats.
b. Puma-esque sneakers.
c. Black stiletto boots.
d. Red leather platforms.

3. Your crush has a crush on someone else/ You:
a. Find a *new* crush.
b. Cry a little, then gracefully accept defeat.
c. Trust your gut and wait it out—he'll come around.
d. Fight for him.

4. Next to your bed is the following reading material:
a. The latest best-selling paperback novel.
b. A college pamphlet.
c. An astrology guide.
d. A thick classic, like *Crime and Punishment*.

5. When you meet someone new, you:
a. Talk about the news or latest celeb gossip.
b. Make small talk.
c. Immediatley try to figure that person out.
d. Go around the room introducing her to new people.

6. It's fourth quarter and you're down by one point, You:
a. Are the only one playing who's not nervous.
b. Think, it's just a game.
c. Pray.
d. Go for a game-winning shot if you're open.

Scoring

If you get a tie, you have dual powers.

mostly a's: VERSATILITY

You have the special ability to adapt to any situation. Hardly anything fazes you, because you're so good at thinking on your feet. So whether it's a party, the classroom, a football game, or a debate, you feel right at home—and in control.

mostly b's: X-RAY VISION

You are a realist—you see things as they truly are. Your ability to decipher everything you see helps you make smart decisions and keeps you from getting hurt, because you know the drill.

mostly c's: INTUITION

You get a vibe, and you go with it. Your instinct helps you in every kind of situation, like knowing the trends before they're cool, winning over teachers, and knowing when that cute guy has a crush on you.

mostly d's: COURAGE

Wow, Supergirl! There's nothing you're afraid of, and people rely on you because of your mental toughness. Sure, you've been through a few hard times, but there's nothing you can't handle now—and that makes you an inspiration to everyone around you.

ARE YOU HIGH MAINTENANCE?

Find out if you're a pain in the tush or totally laid-back.

1. It's raining! Your:

a. Find the biggest puddle to jump in.
b. Pull out your trusty umbrella.
c. Run for the nearest Starbucks.
d. Scream and immediately head home—your hair and makeup are ruined, and now your day is too!

2. If you break a nail, you:

a. Nails? What nails? You bit them off and spit them out yesterday.
b. File it down—the natural look is in!
c. Walk into the nearest salon for an emergency appointment.
d. Page your on-call manicurist.

3. At a party, you:

a. Just drink the store-brand soda.
b. Grab a Coke from the fridge.
c. Ask the cutest guy around to get you a glass of punch.
d. Order the hostess to fetch you a Perrier—and make it snappy!

4. Dressing up for you is:

a. A denim jacket and track pants.
b. Jeans and a sequined tank.
c. Your favorite sexy top and low-slung slim pants.
d. A little black dress, heels, and a blow-out at the salon.

a. Nelly Furtado.
b. Pink.
c. Beyoncé Knowles.
d. Christina Aguilera.

a. Let 'em talk—she can have him.
b. Join the conversation.
c. Tell him that you need to talk.
d. Throw a drink in her face and tell her to stay away from your man.

Scoring

1 point for every a, 2 for b's, 3 for c's, and 4 for d's.

6-10 points: **DEATH BEFORE DIVAHOOD**

You're the type of girl who's comfortable rolling out of bed and just living life (ahh!). But beware: You're *so* content that other, more diva-ish types could try to take advantage of you. So don't you dare let other people be the boss of you, okay?

11-15 points: **99.44% NON-DIVA**

You know how to happily roll with the punches. You're comfortable being yourself and even know how to compromise with the people around you. But you're nobody's doormat, either.

16-19 points: **BEING CONSIDERED FOR DIVAHOOD**

You're über-confident, so it makes sense that you like to do things your way. Independent thinking is great, but so is respecting and appreciating *other* people's brilliance. Sit back and let your friends have a say sometimes too!

20-24 points: **DOYENNE OF DIVAS**

You want to be your best, and you won't stop until you are. That makes you driven—but some people see it as pushy. So try not to pop a blood vessel when things don't go your way. Instead of throwing a tantrum, try to see the humor in the situation.

ARE YOU TOO SUPERFICIAL?

Look a little bit closer and see for yourself just how image-conscious you really are!

1. A hairdresser gives your friend an awful cut. You:
a. Say, "It looks fine—and it'll grow."
b. Suggest she invest in a cool hat.
c. Make fun of her behind her back.

2. Your nana offers you her brown 1980 Chevy. You:
a. Are psyched to have your own car.
b. Spend your b-day money on a paint job.
c. Say, "Thanks, but no thanks."

3. Your yearbook photo is totally hideous. You:
a. Get bummed but think, Does *anyone* look good in them?
b. Retake pictures to get a better shot.
c. Get airbrushed.

4. You oversleep for school, so you:
a. Skip your shower to arrive on time.
b. Shower, pull your hair back, and arrive 15 minutes late.
c. Skip class so you can get fully ready.

5. You would never date a guy who:
a. Was obnoxious to your friends.
b. Had less-than-popular friends.
c. Didn't dress like Ashton and/or drive a nice car.

6. You work out at the gym so that you can:
a. Get that natural endorphin high.
b. Be part of the whole gym "scene."
c. Look hot in tight jeans and shirts.

When it comes to looks, you...

mostly a's: Don't care ›

Spend time primping and preening? No way! You see beyond the external and think that *character* matters more than looks. But most of the world, alas, *does* base judgments on what they see. So sometimes—like on interviews—you'll have to take some extra care to look as confident as you feel.

mostly b's: Kinda care

Sure, you'll take a second glance in the mirror. But you also know where to draw the line, and you don't obsess over the way you—or others—look. Keep putting that extra effort into looking good if it helps you *feel* good and gives you a confidence boost, but don't let yourself get carried away.

mostly c's: Care a lot

Put that mirror down! It's fine to look your best on the out-side—if you feel as good on the *inside*. If you don't, focus on things you're good at (tennis? cooking?) to remind yourself that you've got substance! And remember: You'll miss out on a lot if you judge people based only on their looks.

HOW MATURE ARE YOU?

Are you wise beyond your years, or are you just a wise-butt?

1. Your parents leave town for the weekend. So you:

a. Throw a huge party and try to make sure nothing gets broken.
b. Get a group of friends together for a last-minute sleepover.
c. Invite a friend over for a movie.
d. Clean the house and water the plants, just like they asked.

2. When you like a guy, how do you usually let him know it? You:

a. Have your best friend tell him.
b. Play hard to get and ignore him.
c. Try to go to his favorite places and "bump into him" a lot.
d. Get to know him first, and let the relationship slowly evolve.

3. You get $100 for your birthday from rich Aunt Janie (wa-ha-hooey!). You:

a. Spend it on shoes.
b. Treat your best friends to dinner—sushi for four, please!
c. Buy a hot new perfume, then save the rest for a rainy day.
d. Save up for a new CD burner.

4. If you were caught in class without your homework, you would:

a. Concoct an elaborate lie about how your bag was stole.
b. Stall by saying you left it in your locker, then do it at lunch.
c. Explain why you didn't finish it.
d. You *always* do your homework!

a. Stay out—if you're already in trouble, you may as well live it up.
b. Go home in an hour, but prepare to face consequences.
c. Just get home *fast*—calling might make it into a bigger issue.
d. Call home and explain.

a. Babysitting, mowing lawns—any hourly job that gives you freedom.
b. Waitressing—the flexible schedule lets you have a life.
c. A retail job (discount alert!).
d. An internship with your own computer and voice mail!

Scoring

Add 1 point for each a, 2 for b's, 3 for c's, and 4 for d's.

6-11 points: BABY FACE

"Hello, NBC? We've got a new sitcom for you. It's based on the life of this funny, mischievous girl." Um, that'd be *you*. But while the outrageous situations you get into would be great on TV, they can make *real* life tough. So, go ahead and act like a kid—just be responsible enough to learn from your mistakes.

12-19 points: PRESENT PERFECT

You're responsible enough to know who you are and where you're going (no, not like Arby's—like college!), but there's still a side of you that appreciates Pop-Tarts and old friends. And that's why people love you—you act your (appropriate) age!

20-24 points: GOING ON 30

Let's see...your parents trust you, your friends love your advice, and your teachers consider you a godsend. Yup, you've got it together! Have you ever noticed how people call you an "old soul"? But don't forget to play in the sprinklers sometimes—when life gets serous, know how to have fun!

ARE YOU WEIRD?

Learn to love your inner freakazoid... We know she's in there somewhere.

1. Your new teacher asks everyone about their hobbies. You knit, run, and watch lots of movies. You say:

a. "I watch foreign movies no one's heard of—like *Audition*, where this girl cuts off this guy's leg and puts all these needles in his eyes."

b. "I run cross-country, and, oh, I also like to knit sometimes."

c. "I like to go jogging."

2. You're eating breakfast on the go, and you wind up spilling grape juice all over your top, so you:

a. Wear it like that and tell everyone you got into a horrible accident with Grimace in the parking lot of McDonald's on your way to school.

b. Cover it up with your skater friend's tee. (He always wears at least two.)

c. Change into the spare shirt you keep in your locker *at all times.*

3. Your assignment: Do an in-class presentation on Shirley Temple. Naturally, you:

a. Wear a totally outrageous polka-dot dress, put your hair in tight curls, and tap-dance.

b. Show some key movie clips, and bring in Sprite and grenadine to serve the drink named after her.

c. Give a moving speech about her life, from her child-star days to her job with the State Department.

4. Which of the following makeup products would you be most likely to impulse-buy?

a. Turquoise rainbow-glitter mascara.

b. Super-shiny magenta nail polish.

c. A nice rose lipstick that's just a shade lighter than your lips.

5. During truth or dare, you're dared to "sleepwalk" into your friend's brother's room. You:

a. Barge into his room, add some loud talking and snoring for extra effect, and dramatically bump into things (including him).
b. Slowly open his door, take a few steps in, then run back out.
c. Ask for a truth instead.

6. If you found out you just won the Volkswagen of your choice, you'd ask for:

a. "One of those old vans from the '70s—preferably with a shag carpet."
b. "A Beetle—but in slate gray. None of that wacky bright green for me."
c. "A Jetta."

7. Which celebrity do you look at and go, "You know, when I'm famous, I want to be like *her*"?

a. Gwen Stefani
b. Drew Barrymore
c. Mandy Moore

Scoring

Give yourself 1 point for every a, 2 for every b, and 3 for every c. Now add 'em up!

7-11 points: Truly bizarro

You know how people say, "You're insane!"? Well, you're *not*. But you act the way you want to act without worrying what other people think. That's considered weird because most *adults* don't even dare to go their own way. Basically, you're brave. So how can you be more normal? Don't even *try*! As long as you're not getting yourself in trouble, you're being normal… for you! Weird on, CosmoGIRL!

12-16 points: Classically strange

Sure, you might break-dance in the cafeteria, but you save the moves for when the vice principal isn't on lunch duty. When "normal" is needed (i.e., in class or on a job interview), you can play that role, too. As long as neither way of "acting" stresses you out, you're just doing a good job of expressing yourself honestly. Weirdo!

17-21 points: Weirdly normal

You're the queen of common sense, and we love it. But nobody's perfect, so you might be holding yourself back to *seem* totally together. Look, it's *okay* to bug out over Burt Bacharach or wear an "odd" tee if it's what *you* want to do. So when you want to do something offbeat, think, Who cares if I seem "weird"?! Then go for it!

ARE YOU MOTIVATED?

Turbo Girl...or Turtle Girl? Put your zest to the test!

1. All right! You get paired with your crush for your English class screenplay project. You...

a. Run up to him after class and tell him every detail of your brilliant idea.
b. Tell him you'll start thinking up storylines.
c. Let *him* make the first move. If he writes the whole movie, then he'll *really* be your leading man.

2. The school radio station needs a DJ. When the media teacher asks you to fill the post, you say...

a. You'd be *thrilled* to.
b. You'll think about it for a while. (*Four whole* after-school hours?)
c. No *way*—you'd have to miss *Oprah.*

3. Oh, man—it's two stress-filled days before your make-it-or-break-it biology test. You...

a. Memorize the entire skeletal system in a three-hour power session.
b. Crack your book and make an outline.
c. Complain to your friends that you'll never be able to memorize how this bone is connected to that bone.

4. Your best friend's fitness frenzy is rubbing off on you. You...

a. Show up at her house in your full jogging gear first thing in the morning.
b. Do fifty sit-ups before bed two nights a week.
c. Put on your Pumas and watch beach aerobics on TV.

5. Your parents warn you:
Clean up your bedroom or
kiss your phone privileges
good-bye. You...

a. Morph into a crazy clean-
ing machine, pronto.
b. Take an MTV break, then
pick up the pigsty in time
to beat your friend's phone
curfew.
c. Tell your folks to keep the
cordless: You're not going
near that disaster area.

6. It's finally Friday—but
there's zilch going on for
the weekend. You...

a. Tell your friends to meet at
your house at 7 p.m.
sharp—you've planned a
surprise spa party!
b. Start making plans to
guarantee that *next*
weekend is awesome.
c. Sit at home hoping the
phone will ring.

7. You're freaking out over
paying for your Spring
Break beach trip. You
decide to...

a. Lie about your age and sell
your plasma or your unfer-
tilized eggs.
b. Baby-sit every Friday from
now till then.
c. Announce to relatives that
you'd like to receive
money instead of a gift for
every holiday (please).

8. You log on and...*woo-
hoo!* "You've got mail!" You
hit the reply button...

a. Immediately. You want to
make sure you have more
mail tomorrow.
b. For *some* of the mes-
sages. You don't bother
to answer boring group
e-mails.
c. Later. You save your old
mail and promise yourself
you'll write back someday.
Maybe Saturday?

Scoring

Give yourself three points for every "a" answer, two points for every "b" answer, and one point for every "c" answer.

20 to 24 points: MISS MOTIVATION

You never have to be nagged—even if the mission is de-molding the refrigerator. For superhuman overachievers like yourself, success is a sure thing. But there's something missing from your bright future: *Sleep!* So, how can you chill out? Schedule some downtime—literally. If "goof off" is on your to-do list, you'll feel better about actually doing it.

14 to 19 points: BREAK-TAKER

You're not the type to tune into a *Real World* marathon, but you don't feel the need to do stuff ASAP, either. You get things done, but you're also willing to cut loose and have some fun. Your last-second scrambles can cause excess stress. Allowing extra time for unforeseen snags will cut down on your panic.

8 to 13 points: SERIOUS SLACKER

You're not oblivious to the fact that things need to be done; you're just a master at putting stuff off—and off. But there are times when you need to force yourself into just-do-it mode: If you respond to everything with a no-can-do attitude, you'll be missing out on some pretty amazing life experiences.

CAN YOU TELL A GOOD RISK FROM A BAD ONE ?

1. Woo-hoo! Your friend invites you, a ski virgin, to hit the slopes. You accept. When you get to Mt. Humongo, the first thing you do is...
a. Head for the hardest run. Nothing ventured, nothing gained!
b. Sign up for a lesson. A broken leg is *not* your idea of a fashion statement.
c. Take a seat by the fire at the lodge. You'll leave the daredevil stuff to your friend, Little Miss Super-Skier.

2. Your prankster friends decide to sneak into the guys' locker room, steal their boxers, and run them up the flagpole. You agree to...
a. Plan and execute the maneuver. They call *you* when it's mission impossible.
b. Stand lookout. You want a piece of the fun—without handling the merch.
c. Hear all about it later.

You can't get detention for just listening!

3. One of your fellow cashiers at the Food Mart invites you to her millenn-ium bash, but you won't know a soul there. You say...
a. "Par-*tay*! I can't wait to meet all those new cute guys."
b. "Can I bring my three best friends? We travel as a group."
c. "Um, thanks, but I should keep my parents comp-any—in case the world ends or something."

4. You'll wait on a long line at the amusement park just to get on...
a. The ten-story bungee jump—free fall is so excellent!
b. The log flume ride—you like the splash without the crash.
c. The carousel—now that you're older, it doesn't make you dizzy!

5. After seeing Lauryn Hill in concert, you *know* you want to be a singer. Your plan of action is to...

a. Sign up to sing at open-mike night. Why not go for it?

b. Beg your parents for voice lessons. Your teacher will help you develop your "potential."

c. Sing your heart out in the shower when no one's home—the last thing you need is for your *sister* to make fun of you.

6. The hottest guy you've *ever* seen is hanging with some people from your class. You...

a. March right up, say "hey" to the people you know, and introduce yourself to His Royal Cuteness.

b. Muster the guts to ask one of the people you know to introduce you to him.

c. Avoid eye contact—he probably has a girlfriend. Plus, you don't want him to dis you in front of your classmates.

7. Your parents leave town and give you strict "no party" instructions. At 9 p.m., a group of your pals ring the doorbell, ready to rumba. You...

a. Fling your door open wide and shout, "Let the party begin!"

b. Grab your coat and meet them outside. Maybe you can't host a party, but no parents means no curfew!

c. Hide in the dark and later lie through your braces. "Doorbell? What doorbell? I must have been drying my hair."

Scoring

Give yourself 3 points for every a, 2 points for every b, and 1 point for every c.

17 to 21 points: DAREDEVIL DIVA

You've never met a risk you didn't take, and your spontaneity makes you the life of the party. Once in a while, though, you leap (dive! bungee jump!) before you look and get into trouble.

A little prep work can help: Take a lesson before you ski Mt. Humongo, and make sure the girl with Mr. Perfect isn't his girlfriend before you slip him your number. You'll still have a thrillsville life—just without the occasional blush-producing blooper (or bone-breaking accident).

12 to 16 points: REASONABLE RISKER

With your great sense of adventure, you have the guts to try just about anything—within reason. But you also know when it's time to be careful, like when you strap on a helmet before climbing onto the back of your friend's motorbike. Feed your courage by reveling in past successes.

7 to 11 points: SAFE SISTER

Sometimes your "that-could-be-way-too-embarrassing" radar keeps you from doing things you might enjoy, like trying out for the soccer team. Start by taking little risks—accept an invite you'd normally nix or say hi to someone you don't know well. Soon, taking a chance will get much easier.

How to take THE PLUNGE:

Making positive changes in your life means taking chances. Scared? Try these tips:

Set your goal. Close your eyes and visualize what you want—and how great it will feel when you get it.
Start small. Break goals into steps and tackle one step at a time.
Get inspired. Talk to or read about someone who's accomplished a similar goal and learn from her experiences.
Expect mistakes. Just figure out what went wrong and think about what you could do differently next time.

WHAT KIND OF FRIEND ARE YOU?

This, CosmoGIRL!, is why you are loved so much!

1. When your best friend gets dumped, you:

a. Spend hours listening to her.
b. Help her craft a letter telling the loser why she's glad he's gone.
c. Take her out for ice cream.
d. Share your dating disasters.

2. Your best friend has a big date. She's nervous so you:

a. Help her get ready.
b. Tell her he's lucky to be with her.
c. Go shopping with her in search of an awesome dress.
d. Lend her your sexiest jeans.

3. You hear a scandalous secret about someone. You:

a. Tell the person everyone's talking about her.
b. Take it to your grave.
c. Tell everyone to stop blabbing.
d. Let everyone pry it out of you

4. Which of the following colors best reflects your true personality? It is:

a. Purple—calm and collected.
b. Red—strong and determined.
c. Orange—dynamic and fun.
d. Blue—soothing and easy-going.

5. When your friends are hanging out, you:

a. Play the role of Dear Abby.
b. Laugh hard at everyone's jokes—even if they're bombs.
c. Suggest taking a road trip.
d. Pick up the tab.

6. Who is your favorite character on the popular show Friends?

a. Rachel.
b. Either Phoebe or Joey.
c. Monica.
d. Either Ross or Chandler.

Scoring

Did you end up with a tie? Your type totally depends on who your friend is. So read 'em both!

mostly a's: THE CONFIDANTE

You're the person your friends trust the most. They know they can turn to you when they need to vent—no matter what time of day (or night!) it may be. You really, *really* listen—and of course, give thoughtful advice

mostly b's: 100 PERCENT DEVOTED

You're the one who can always be counted on. No matter what happens, you stand behind your friends through thick and thin. It's your true-blue devotion that makes you so popular—when you make a friend, you're that persons friend for life.

mostly c's: THE MOTIVATOR

You're always there to pick up the pieces when things go wrong, or to cheer your friends on when things go *right*. You draw out people's best qualities, which makes them want to follow your lead.

mostly d's: THE GIVER

You're a "what's mine is yours" kind of girl—you go out of your way to share everything from clothes to advice. That selfless attitude is wonderful, but don't let people take advantage of your generosity!

HOW FAR WOULD YOU GO FOR YOUR FRIENDS?

Would you walk on hot coals—or just little pebbles—to be by her side?

1. Your friend has a huge crush. You:

a. Throw a party and invite him—so they can finally hang out.

b. Flatter her when he's within earshot.

c. Help her map out a flirting strategy.

2. When she misses a week of classes before a test, you:

a. Pull an all-nighter to help her cram.

b. Photocopy your notes for her.

c. Buy her a cutesy good-luck pencil.

3. Your crush asks you out, but you already have plans with a friend. You:

a. Ask him for a rain check.

b. See your friend—then meet him later.

c. Reschedule her.

4. You're both interviewing for the same job. You:

a. Withdraw your application.

b. Go for the job and encourage her to too.

c. Say, "May the best woman win!"

5. She can't afford to go on spring break. You:

a. Skip it—and have fun at home together.

b. Lend her $200 in baby-sitting money.

c. Bring her back kitschy souvenirs.

6. She dropped her bracelet in the toilet at school. You:

a. Reach in to get it.

b. Help her find a random contraption to use to fish it out.

c. Crack up with her as she reaches in!

You'd go...

mostly a's: ABOVE AND BEYOND

Your unwavering loyalty is impressive! But make sure you go out of your way for friends because you truly want to—not because you think you *have* to. True friends will understand that you need to put *yourself* first sometimes. Because being a good friend doesn't mean meeting their needs at all costs— it means being there for someone who's there for *you* too.

mostly b's: ALL THE WAY

You love your friends, and you're there to help them as much as you can. You have a finely tuned sense of when it's appropriate to drop what you're doing for someone else and when you need to focus on your own needs. You see friend-ship as a two-way street, and the people who are closest to you return the energy you put out for them by being there for you. Put simply, you've learned the fine art of *mutual* respect.

mostly c's: A STEP OR TWO

You enjoy being with your friends—and you'll be there for them as long as doing so doesn't interfere with your own pri-orities or plans. It's good that you don't let yourself get off track, but every once in a while, going out of your way when a friend needs you is just the right thing to do. You know that whole saying about a friend in need being a friend indeed? Well, it's true!

ANALYZE THIS!

Grab a pen and see what your handwriting reveals about you.

People don't have to read your journal to discover your inner secrets—they can find out just by looking at your history notes! "Huh?" you say? Well, it has to do with your script: Your strokes, slants, and structure hint at different aspects of your character. Experts believe emotional signals connect with those mechanical commands that shoot from the brain to control the movements guiding your pen. So write the sentence below in script to find out what you're revealing.

You and your silly monkey do not go home to the zoo on Friday.

Look at your *t*. Is it...

To

Crossed up high
You're full of confidence and ambition, so you continually set the bar higher for yourself. That strong sense of self will lead you to success and happiness.

to

Crossed low
You evaluate yourself every chance you get. This helps you catch your mistakes before others even notice them—but be sure you don't focus only on your flaws.

Look at your *m*. Does it have...

monkey

Round humps

You're at the top of your game when you take time to learn the facts you need to know. And once you've got that info down, it'll stay with you practically forever!

monkey

Jagged humps

You have a lightning-fast mind, which helps when cramming for exams or memorizing people's names. But take time to review the stuff you want to know long term.

Look at your *o*. Is it...

zoo

Looped to the right

You're a private person who's great at keeping secrets. Since opening up is hard for you, if you want to get stuff off your chest, try writing a letter to a friend.

zoo

Looped to the left

You're good at hiding your anxiety from others. But an issue can really gnaw at you sometimes, so jot down whatever comes to mind until you identify what's bugging you.

zoo

Double-looped

You tend to tell white lies to spare others' feelings. But you may cause more harm than good: People might not trust you when they find out you tell tales.

zoo

Open, no loops

You give your honest opinion—whether anyone asks or not. But that can be hurtful, so speak up when necessary, but be sure to think about what you're saying first.

Look at your *y*. Does it have a...

Big low loop
You take what people say at face value, which is great. But others aren't always right—so ask questions to learn the facts. In the process, you'll gain more knowledge.

Right upstroke
You tend to let tension build up. Unload some of your stress by doing something physical—try heading out for a jog or shooting some hoops to really unwind.

Slight or no loop
Your fear of getting hurt makes it hard for you to trust. Let down your guard by sharing small things with those you're close to and slowly working up to the big stuff.

Look at your *slant*. Does it go...

To the right
You feel everything deeply—whether it's happiness or sadness. Be sure you don't let emotions get the best of you—share your thoughts with an even-keeled friend.

To the left
You care deeply about others, but you can come across as aloof because you're not that demonstrative. So be sure to tell people what you're feeling more often

Upward
You have a great, balanced approach to life and decision making. Your ability to see the bright side of things helps you rise above any obstacles you face.

Want *write*-on improvements?
Build the character traits you want by adjusting your handwriting. Like, if you cross your *t's* higher, you'll *feel* more confident in 30 days. Try it!

GET INTO YOUR ELEMENT!

Chinese philosophers believed every personality could be linked with one of five natural elements. Take this quiz to find yours!

1. If you joined the drama club at your school, you'd most likely be:

a. The director, leading the way.
b. The star of the show, of course!
c. The stage manager, taking care of all the actors' needs.
d. On the design crew, making sets and figuring out how to set them up.
e. The visionary playwright.

2. When you're channel surfing, which show always makes you stop and put down the remote control and watch it?

a. *The Apprentice.*
b. *The E! True Hollywood Story.*
c. A movie on Lifetime.
d. *CSI.*
e. *Joan of Arcadia.*

3. If your best friends had to describe you with only one word, which of the following do you think they'd probably choose?

a. Competitive
b. Dramatic.
c. Nurturing.
d. Organized.
e. Introspective.

4. You'd feel the most relaxed and be the happiest in which one of these environments?

a. A redwood forest, surrounded by the biggest and tallest of trees.
b. The hot, sun-soaked tropics.
c. A flower-filled meadow.
d. On top of a snow-covered mountain.
e. Near an ocean or a lake.

You find a hundred-dollar bill on the street. You

a. Invest it so you'll make more.
b. Spend it all immediately.
c. Give it to a homeless person.
d. Figure out how to track down its owner—ASAP.
e. Wonder why you found it and what you were destined to do with it.

It's winter break. Which class is making an assignment would you actually enjoy working on during your vacation?

a. Business.
b. Public speaking.
c. Art.
d. Math.
e. Philosophy.

scoring: Which letter did you circle most often? Match up that letter with your element below!

Mostly a's: wood
color: **green**
symbol: **dragon**
planet: **Jupiter**
your personality: You always aim high, looking to grow and expand—just like a tree. But at the same time your feet are firmly rooted and you approach your goals in a patient, rational way. Plus, your competitive and assertive nature and your quick problem-solving skills make you an excellent leader. It's hard for you to convey deep emotions, but it's easy for you to express yourself in a power position.
power tip: Keep a small tree like a bonsai in your room to help enhance your inner wood energy.

Mostly b's: fire
color: **red**
symbol: **phoenix**
planet: **Mars**
your personality: Like a fire, you're bright, intriguing, and quick to grab people's attention. You approach everything you do with passion and enthusiasm and are always up for trying new and adventurous things. You thrive on variety, so you can sometimes get frustrated or impatient when things become routine. Your friends love being around you because of your courage, charisma, and sociable energy!
power tip: Put a red night-light in your room to strengthen that fiery energy of yours.

Mostly c's: earth
color: **yellow**
symbol: **cauldron**
planet: **Saturn**
your personality: Like the earth's soil, you're very nurturing. You make a trustworthy, reliable friend and always have a shoulder ready for anyone to cry on. When problems come your way, you tend to work them out in a fair, practical manner. Although you worry a lot about things you can't control, you feel safe and calm when surrounded by family or close friends. You're low-key, you don't get worked up easily, and overall, you're very...well, down-to-earth!
power tip: Grow a flowering plant in a terra-cotta pot in your room to nurture your inner earth energy.

Mostly d's: metal
color: white
symbol: tiger
planet: Venus
your personality: You're persistent, and once you make up your mind, you're hard to bend—like metal itself! Very organized and disciplined, you'll see a task through to the end, no matter how long it takes. You have inner and outer strength and enjoy physical challenges. You see life as a puzzle to be solved logically, and you love to analyze new ideas and people. Use your self-control to keep that negativity you sometimes give off in check.
power tip: Display a small dish of coins in your room to help activate your inner metal energy.

Mostly e's: water
color: blue
symbol: tortoise
planet: Mercury
your personality: You're deep and mysterious, like the ocean. As an emotional, sensitive, and spiritual soul, you're constantly in search of honesty and truth in life. You enjoy spending introspective time alone to think and dream. You also have keen intuition, which makes you a great listener. But you'd much rather daydream than deal with some of life's harsher realities, like facing conflict.
power tip: If you set up a small aquarium with fish in your room, it will help reinforce your inner water energy.

WHAT'S YOUR CUP O' JOE?

See exactly where your personality falls on the beverage menu!

1. At parties, you usually:
a. Talk to the shy girl.
b. Wish you'd stayed in with your friends.
c. Chill out in a side room with the coolest people there.
d. Invent games!

2. What's your most prized possession?
a. Photos of your family and friends.
b. Your journal.
c. Your poetry.
d. Your goofy pet rock collection.

3. The one TV show you make sure never to miss is:
a. *7th Heaven.*
b. *Buffy the Vampire Slayer* repeats.
c. *Joan of Arcadia.*
d. *One Tree Hill.*

4. Where did you buy your favorite coat this year?
a. At a cute local boutique.
b. In a high-tech sporting goods store.
c. At an antique fair.
d. On eBay.

5. Which major appeals to you?
a. Social work or medicine.
b. Law, business, or communications.
c. Art or philosophy.
d. I'll create my own major.

6. What would you be most likely to get detention for?
a. Talking in class.
b. Cutting class.
c. Refusing to play hockey in gym.
d. Leading a sit-in to protest school policy.

You're like a...

You're full of natural sugar! You're a lovable, genuine, and positive presence. People turn to you when they need a sympathetic ear because of your sensitivity and knack for bringing comfort to tough situations.

mostly b's: Espresso forte

You're robust. You're strong in flavor and don't need excessive froufrou in your life. You may seem too bitter for some people, but those who *really* know you appreciate your no-nonsense attitude—you get things done and tell it like it is.

mostly c's: Kenya AA

You're mysterious and exotic. Deeply spiritual, you seek out knowledge, understanding, and adventure—which makes you anything but ordinary! People rely on you to help them see things from a new perspective.

mostly d's: Iced mint-o-chino

You're eclectic. People describe you as quirky and full of surprises because your presence sparks things up in any room. Spending time with you is a totally refreshing way to amp up even the *most* mundane situations!

WHAT'S YOUR BEAUTY STYLE?

Whether you're catching waves, cuties, or rays (or all three), take our quiz and find out which summer beauty goodies are *perfect* for your personality.

1. Your favorite treat on a really hot summer day is:

a. Sorbet.
b. Mocha Frappuccino.
c. Fruit yogurt smoothie.

2. If you could score your dream car, you'd pick:

a. A sleek import with a sunroof.
b. A convertible.
c. An SUV.

3. The star you'd most like to trade lives with for a day is:

a. Natalie Portman.
b. Beyoncé Knowles.
c. Cameron Diaz.

4. Between bands at an outdoor summer music festival, you're most likely to be found:

a. Buying concert T-shirts for all of your friends.
b. Scoping out ways to sneak backstage to meet the band.
c. Playing a game of Frisbee with the hot guys on the next blanket.

5. You're so predictable—people laugh at the fact that you:

a. Always pack a cardigan in case you happen to get cold.
b. Take four hours to get ready, even if you're just going to the grocery store.
c. Love to win at everything—even silly card games like Go Fish!

a. Prince William—gorgeous eyes, sexy accent...he's a real prince!
b. Orlando Bloom—rugged good looks and always dressed to kill!
c. LeBron James—rockin' bod, major talent, and a Nike contract!

a. Doing volunteer work.
b. At the mall scooping up the latest hair stuff and makeup—and a few outfits too.
c. Working out early when the gym's not so crowded.

a. J. Crew—they have so many adorable bathing suits.
b. Sephora—they have the coolest new hair and makeup stuff.
c. Niketown—they have gear for everything from hiking to surfing.

a. Romance—you love movies with sappy (but happy) endings.
b. New releases—who cares about all the old boring ones?!
c. Action—fast-paced movies loaded with cool stunts are the best way to get an adrenaline rush.

Scoring

Find your score below (isn't it scary how well we know you?).

mostly a's: Preppy

You always look put together, but you're not fussy about your makeup. You stick to soft, girlie colors that look natural and blend perfectly with your skin tone.

mostly b's: Glam

You have a knack for finding the hottest, newest stuff before anyone else. Plus, you choose cool things—and *always* know exactly which products celebs are using.

mostly c's: Sporty

You want a look that won't get in the way of your active lifestyle, so you pick makeup that won't give you the slip when you dive into the pool or get a little sweaty.

WHAT KIND OF PROM DRESS FITS YOUR PERSONALITY?

Discover which stylish getup is just right for you!

1. What did you do last Friday night?
a. Baby-sat.
b. Hosted a *Sex and the City* DVD-athon.
c. Went to some older kid's party.
d. Rallied a crew for some karaoke.

2. If you could change your life for a day, which of these celebs would you want to be?
a. Mandy Moore.
b. Beyoncé Knowles.
c. Scarlett Johansson.
d. Gwen Stefani.

3. Which shoes do you like most?
a. Ballet flats.
b. Stiletto heels with ankle straps.
c. Mid-calf black leather boots.
d. Knee-high red pleather boots.

4. Your ideal prom date would wear:
a. A classic dark tux.
b. A dark suit with a funky silk tie.
c. A coat and tails.
d. A hilarious baby blue tux—with a ruffly shirt to boot!

5. Your friends love you because:
a. You're always sweet and sincere.
b. You know how to make things fun.
c. You give the all-time best advice.
d. You'll try anything.

6. What do you sleep in?
a. Pastel-colored night-gowns.
b. Perfectly broken-in T-shirts.
c. Matching top-and-bottom ensembles.
d. Nada!

You're like a...

mostly a's: Princess ball gown

You pride yourself on being a supergirlie girl! Sweet and cute, you're known for putting in the kind of extra effort that will always make you look classically feminine. You also appreciate and pay close attention to small details that others might miss.

mostly b's: Short cocktail dress

You're the life of every party! Carefree and confident, you make everyone feel comfortable when they're around you. Like your dress type, you're endearingly flirty and charming — and your spunky personality is infectious!

mostly c's: Long, sleek gown

You're sophisticated beyond your years! Like this classic dress, you tend to be in the spotlight. But not because you're loud or clamoring for attention. Your quiet elegance speaks for itself, and that maturity and glamour attracts many people to you for advice.

mostly d's: Look-at-me dress

Your style is all your own! You have a natural knack for mixing and matching skirts and tops, combing thrift stores, and reconfiguring dresses to make them look totally new and unique. Some people think your eccentricity makes you too far out there, but that's exactly the reaction you want to get!

ARE YOU SUPERSTITIOUS?

Put down that Magic 8 Ball long enough to see if you rely too much on fate!

1. You're wearing a new shirt when your crush finally asks you out. You:
a. Don't wash it so it'll retain its power.
b. Wear it when you need a boost of luck.
c. Don't think twice.

2. A black cat prances directly in front of you. You:
a. Turn around and find a new route.
b. Gasp loudly, then laugh at yourself.
c. Make kissy-kissy noises at it.

3. A friend mentions that you're a shoo-in for class president. You:
a. Are sure she just jinxed the vote.
b. Cross your fingers and hope so.
c. Thank her.

4. Has the Ouija board ever freaked you out?
a. It's not that it freaks me out; I just value it so much that I only use it sparingly.
b. Once or twice.
c. Nah.

5. You don't talk about the future because you:
a. Think fate might play a joke on you.
b. Never know what might come up to change things.
c. Don't plan ahead.

6. Your compact shatters. You:
a. Brace yourself for years of bad luck.
b. Figure a small mirror can't do *that* much damage.
c. Are annoyed you need to replace it.

you're a...

Your intuition tells you it's better to be safe than sorry.
This superstitious side is a reflection of your faith in higher
powers. But don't sell yourself short; your fortune also owes a
lot to your talent, skills, and hard work. Fate isn't the only
force that shapes your life—*you* shape it too!

You aren't immune to the mysterious allure of rituals. But
you tend to tap into fate only for an extra boost of luck—not
because you think it'll be the one thing that actually deter-
mines your future. You realize chance plays a role in life but
know it's what you do and don't do that really matters.

You scoff at superstition. No one's going to catch you
avoiding sidewalk cracks! With your logical disposition, you
think you're the master of your own destiny. And that's great,
because you know how to rely on yourself. Just don't judge
others who believe a little magic helps!

FRIEND FORTUNE TELLER

Use our version of this old childhood game to see what the future holds for your *friendship!*

How to play: Make a copy of this so you can play with a friend. Fill in options for each category below. (Write four good possibilities and one really out-there one!) Then start drawing a spiral in the box below. When your friend yells "stop," stop! Count the lines across the spiral, then, starting at the letter F below, move that number of spaces (so if it's four, you'll land on E); cross off E, then, starting at N, keep moving four spaces through the category lines top to bottom. Go through college, career, reunion, city, crush, crazy things, and back to FRIEND, crossing off options until only one is left per group. And that, CosmoGIRL!, is how your true friendship "future" will be revealed!

How close you'll live to each other...

| Flight Away | Room together | In the same city | Extremely far away | Next state over | Down the block |

which college you'll attend

_____
_____
_____
_____

which career you'll have

_____
_____
_____
_____

where you'll have an annual reunion

_____
_____
_____
_____

which city you'll live in

_____
_____
_____
_____
_____

celeb crush you'll meet and date

_____
_____
_____
_____
_____

craziest things you'll do together

_____
_____
_____
_____
_____

WHAT COLOR IS YOUR AURA?

Take this quiz and unlock the secret to your inner self!

Directions: **Answer each question in all six groups below and write in** yes **or** no **on the line provided. Be honest and say what you believe you truly** *are*, **not how you'd** *like* **to be. When you finish, check the next page to discover your aura. Ready to get glowing?**

1.
I'd rather take action than discuss plans.

I can get angry fast, but I get over it quickly too.

It's pretty hard for me to express my feelings.

Life is about the physical, not the spiritual.

I prefer concrete ideas to abstract ones.

2.
I crave independence and hate being tied down.

I'm often involved in a lot of projects at once.

I truly believe I can help to improve the world.

I love performing in front of an audience.

I feel I was put here to be important or famous.

3.
I'm very sensitive and aware of others' feelings.

I'm emotional and I tend to cry easily.

I hate dealing with conflict or confrontation.

I feel guilty if I have to say no to someone.

Friends depend on me for a shoulder to cry on.

4.

I enjoy being in charge and delegating work.

_____

I tend to be a perfectionist about most things.

_____

I like things to be organized and well planned.

_____

I love doing competitive activities or sports.

_____

I want a powerful job that pays a lot of money.

_____

5.

I tend to get frustrated if I'm not having fun.

_____

I am optimistic and almost always smiling.

_____

I have lots of energy and detest sitting still.

_____

I'm always told I have a great sense of humor.

_____

I love doing things on the spur of the moment.

_____

6.

I often try to push beyond my physical limits.

_____

I'm always the first to accept any kind of dare.

_____

I love heart-racing things like roller coasters.

_____

There are few things that I'm afraid of.

_____

I'm a risk-taker and I live for adventure.

_____

What's an aura?

It's a group of invisible bands of colored light that surround all living things. Each color has been found to relate to certain personality traits.

Scoring: Tally up your yeses from each group of questions. The group with the most yeses is your aura. Match that group number with its corresponding color below. Have a tie? You have a *combination* aura—your personality reflects more than one color. But whether you have just one aura or several of them, what's important is that it's the essence of *you!*

#1: Red

Personality

With your zest and self-confidence, you live in the here and now. You like to experience the world through taste, touch, and smell, and are happiest when working.

School

When confronted with a difficult problem, you face it with determination. You never let it go unsolved, no matter how long it takes to figure out.

Love

It can be hard for you to open up since you're a very private person. You need someone secure who won't misinterpret your independence.

Career

Your ideal job is one where you control the outcome and have something tangible to show for your work, like being a *chef*, *surgeon*, or *carpenter*.

#2: Violet

Personality

You're a visionary and a dreamer who feels you were put here to do something great. Your flair for the dramatic and your strong charisma will help you make a lasting impact on the world.

School

You love getting involved as a leader in many clubs and take on extra-credit assignments.

Love

You're passionate, but you get so busy inspiring others that you don't have much time for love. You need someone to recognize your vision and work beside you to achieve it.

Career

You'll get the most satisfaction by working for yourself in a job where you feel you make a difference, such as being a *teacher*, *politician*, or *musician*.

#3: Blue

Personality

As a born caretaker, your warmth and intuition help you nurture those around you. In life you follow your heart and believe that everyone should be accepted.

School

Since you're emotional, you stress out easily. But when you quietly sit and get centered, you're always able to regroup and do what needs to be done.

Love

Relationships are your top priority and you get unhappy when you're not in one. You're happiest spending a lot of time with one committed person.

Career

You work best in one-on-one situations and are drawn to fields where you take care of others, such as *nursing*, *psychology*, or *counseling*.

#4: Green

Personality

You're a high-achiever whose aim is to take on the world. You love being in control and hate to be wrong. Your quick thinking and competitive nature will help you meet any goal that you set for yourself.

School

Because you can't stand to fail, you'll push yourself incredibly hard to always be number one. You are a fast learner and love a good mental challenge.

Love

With such high standards, you may find it hard to meet your match. You need someone as goal-oriented and driven as you.

Career

You would thrive in the high-profile, lucrative role of a *stockbroker*, *CEO*, or *salesperson*, or by working solo as an *entrepreneur*.

#5: Yellow

Personality

You feel life's too short to take too seriously, so you seek out things that make you happy. You're fun-loving, energetic, and like to bring joy to those around you.

School

You'd rather be playing, but when you must work, you rely on creativity and humor to help develop unique ideas.

Love

You love to flirt, and since you need freedom, it scares you to be tied down. But once you do find that person who makes you feel safe, you're very loyal.

Career

Variety is key, so you'll probably have many jobs in your life, but all of them will let you have fun. Consider being an *actress*, *writer*, or *comedian*.

#6: Orange

Personality

Physical challenges don't faze you one bit, and you feel most alive when faced with adventure or danger. You're a thrill-seeking daredevil who prefers to be constantly on the go.

School

You attack each test or project with intensity, analyzing all the possible solutions and then jumping right into action.

Love

Only another adventurer will do—you can challenge each other and live life in the fast lane!

Career

You need a high-risk job with flexible hours so you can travel and find adventure too. Think: *forensic detective*, *stunt double*, or *police officer*.

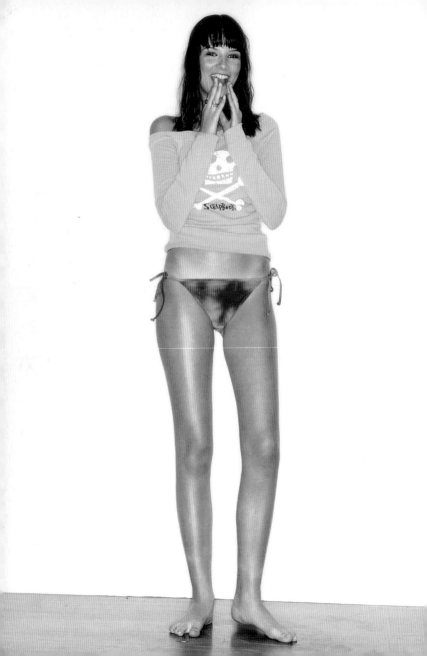

TIME TO FENG SHUI!

So what if you can't pronounce it. This Chinese philosophy can make your room—and your world—a happier place.

1. How is your bed positioned in your room?
a. The head of the bed is right under a window.
b. The headboard is against a wall, and you have a full view of the door—but are not directly across from it.
c. The headboard is along the same wall as the door.

2. Okay, be honest: How would you describe the clutter in your bedroom?
a. Almost nonexistent. You're a neat freak!
b. You try to clean regularly, but somehow it always seems to pile up again.
c. You haven't seen your floor in ages.

3. How many electronic items in your bedroom are plugged in?
a. Three or four, and they're scattered all around the room.
b. No more than two or three, and they're all at least 3 feet away from your bed.
c. Tons, and a bunch of them surround your bed.

4. When you're sitting at your desk:
a. You have your back to the door.
b. You have a blank wall less than 3 feet in front of you.
c. You have a clear view of the main doorway to your room.

5. Your bedroom walls are covered with:
a. Music, movie, and TV posters.
b. Shelves of dolls and/or things from your past.
c. A mix of photos of friends, family, and some celebs.

6. Your closet doors:
a. Open and close easily *and* don't have any mirrors or pictures.
b. Have mirrors hanging on the front of them.
c. Get stuck or jammed all the time in their tracks or on their hinges.

Key:

By following feng shui to move items to certain places, you can create a balanced environment that will influence all aspects of your life. Can't move things to their optimal positions? Try our quick fixes.

1. THE BED: Optimal answer is *b*

Why: If it faces your door, you'll be calmer and more serene, since no one will be able to sneak in or startle you. Chose *a* or *c*? Set up a mirror in the room so that you can see the reflection of your door from your bed.

2. THE CLUTTER: Optimal answer is *a*

Why: Clean, organized areas sharpen your mental clarity. Chose *b* or *c*? If you really can't stay neat, hang a set of wind chimes over the most cluttered area in your room. In feng shui, chimes attract attention and help to focus you.

3. THE ELECTRONIC ITEMS: Optimal answer is *b*

Why: Electronically charged items sap your internal energy. Chose *a* or *c*? Move your gadgets as far from the bed as you can. Put them in a cabinet when they're not in use.

4. THE DESK: Optimal answer is *c*

Why: A door view opens a path to leadership opportunities. Chose *a* or *b*? Prop a mirror on your desk to see the reflection of the door behind you, or hang a picture that has depth (like a landscape) on the wall in front of you.

5. THE WALLS: Optimal answer is *c*

Why: Images of familiar faces lead to better communication. Chose *a* or *b*? Can't part with your past or your posters? Find a happy medium: Pack up half of them and replace the rest with pictures of your friends and family.

6. THE CLOSET: Optimal answer is *a*

Why: Clean, free-moving doors help you make progress. Chose *b* or *c*? Repair doors and cover mirrors with plain white fabric so you won't get stuck in a rut.

HOW MUCH FUN ARE YOU?

Find out if you're the cowgirl who knows how to get the party started! (Yee-haw!)

1. What are you doing for April Fools' Day?
a. Nothing. April Fools' Day is for kids.
b. Putting salt in the sugar bowl and sugar in the salt shaker.
c. Punking *all* day!

2. Your ideal birthday plans are:
a. A whole day of pampering yourself.
b. Having dinner with a bunch of really close friends.
c. A blowout party that goes on all night!

3. When the kids you baby-sit get way too hyper, you:
a. Get the oldest kid to help you calm them.
b. Play tag until they're exhausted.
c. Reverse roles and go kooky on *them*.

4. What's your top career priority?
a. Helping people so you can make a difference in the world.
b. Making big bucks.
c. Finding ways to make the most of your creativity.

5. When your last Friday class gets out early, you:
a. Get a head start on your homework.
b. Relax at home.
c. Round up the girls to hang at your place.

6. It's family reunion time. You:
a. Help your mom make potato salad.
b. Catch up with your favorite cousins.
c. Crack everyone up with your Grandma Sadie impersonation.

You're a...

mostly a's: Party goer

You're mature and responsible—you don't have to go crazy to have fun, and you rarely give in to peer pressure to do something you don't really want to do. That attitude has earned you trust and respect. But remember: Letting your hair down every now and then is key to staying healthy—emotionally and physically—because it gives you a more well-rounded life. So when *your* inner child wants to come out and play, let her!

mostly b's: Party girl

You like to have fun—without going overboard. You're a master at balancing work and play. And when you want to have a good time, you tend to stick to things that are tried and true. Still, there may be times when you'll get pulled to be more spontaneous and less serious—*or* to sacrifice fun in the name of hard work. When that happens, trust that your level-headed approach will steer you in the right direction.

mostly c's: Party animal

Life's a big party to you—you *make* fun happen! You're silly and creative, and you pride yourself on keeping yourself—and your friends—entertained. But that carefree spirit might make some people think they can't take you seriously or rely on you. So make an effort to show that you can be fun and trustworthy at the same time by following through on your responsibilities at home and school, and with friends.

HOW WELL DO YOU KNOW HER?

Everyone knows about her size-10 1/2 feet and her insane crush on Orlando, but some things you share *only* with your closest friend.

DIRECTIONS: Starting with the right column, answer the first six questions about *yourself*, the next six (pg. 108, left) about your *friend*. Fold over your answers, then pass the book to her. On the left, she'll answer six questions about *you* and six (pg. 108, right) about *herself*. Compare. Is it like you're mind readers? Yay! If not, a few late-night gabfests over Ben & Jerry's will do it!

About Her   About Me

------------------   1. Your/her most   --------------------
                          amazing accom-
------------------   plishment so far: --------------------

------------------   2. The first store at   --------------------
                          the mall you go/she
------------------   goes to: --------------------

------------------   3. Name three items   --------------------
                          in your/her bag right
------------------   now: --------------------

------------------   4. Have you/has she   --------------------
                          ever been in love?
------------------   With who?   --------------------

------------------   5. The last time   --------------------
                          you/she cried was
------------------   because: --------------------

------------------   6. In 10 years, where   --------------------
                          do you see your-
------------------   self/her?   --------------------

About Her		About Me
-----------------	1. Your/her most amazing accomplishment so far:	-----------------
-----------------		-----------------
-----------------	2. The first store at the mall you go/she goes to:	-----------------
-----------------		-----------------
-----------------	3. Name three items in your/her bag right now:	-----------------
-----------------		-----------------
-----------------	4. Have you/has she ever been in love? With who?	-----------------
-----------------		-----------------
-----------------	5. The last time you/she cried was because:	-----------------
-----------------		-----------------
-----------------	6. In 10 years, where do you see yourself/her?	-----------------
-----------------		-----------------

Fold in here to hide your answers and pass this quiz to a friend.